LGBTQ+

&

THE RAINBOW'S TAPESTRY

Liberty Grace

Table of contents:

Introductions:

"The Rainbow's Tapestry: Symbolism, Context, and the Importance of Nuance" is a thought-provoking exploration that delves into the complex realm of rainbow symbolism and raises awareness about the potential dangers of oversimplifying its meaning through exclusive associations with the LGBTQ community.

 This book aims to foster a deeper understanding of the rainbow's multifaceted symbolism and encourages nuanced conversations that honor its diverse interpretations across cultures, religions, and historical contexts.

While the rainbow has gained recognition as a powerful symbol within the LGBTQ community, it is essential to recognize that it holds a broader significance beyond this specific context.

 In this book "The Rainbow's Tapestry," we embark on a journey that uncovers the intricacies of rainbow symbolism, emphasizing the importance of acknowledging its diverse meanings and potential risks associated with oversimplification.

By delving into ancient myths, cultural traditions, and religious narratives, this book unveils the rainbow as a symbol that has resonated throughout human history in various ways. It represents a wide spectrum of interpretations, including hope, promise, divine connection, and natural beauty. Understanding the depth and breadth of its symbolism enriches our appreciation of the rainbow's universal appeal.

"LGBTQ, The Rainbow's Tapestry" explores the potential dangers of reducing the rainbow's symbolism solely to the LGBTQ movement. While acknowledging the significance of the rainbow as a symbol of diversity, inclusivity, and the fight for equal rights, this book raises awareness about the need for a nuanced approach that recognizes and respects its broader cultural, historical, and spiritual associations.

By engaging in thoughtful discourse, this book encourages readers to consider the potential consequences of oversimplification and the unintentional erasure of other interpretations and cultural significance surrounding the rainbow. It highlights the importance of inclusivity and understanding, reminding us to value the richness and complexity of diverse symbolisms without diminishing their power through exclusivity.

"The Rainbow's Tapestry" also examines the potential impact on marginalized communities whose identities and struggles may be overshadowed by a singular interpretation of the rainbow.

Chapter 1:

The Rainbow's Historical and Cultural Significance

- Tracing the historical roots of rainbow symbolism in various cultures and time periods.

- Exploring ancient myths, folklore, and religious narratives that incorporate the rainbow as a powerful symbol.

- Highlighting the rainbow's associations with hope, promise, and divine connection across different cultural contexts.

The rainbow holds a rich historical and cultural significance that spans across civilizations, rooted in ancient myths, folklore, and religious narratives.

Since ancient times, humans have been fascinated by the ethereal beauty and enchanting colors of the rainbow, attributing deep symbolic meaning to this natural phenomenon.

In ancient mythology and folklore, the rainbow often emerges as a bridge connecting the earthly and celestial realms. These myths feature stories of gods and divine beings using the rainbow as a pathway to travel between worlds. In Greek mythology, for instance, Iris, the goddess of the rainbow, acts as a messenger between the gods and mortals, bringing divine messages and blessings. Similar beliefs exist in Norse mythology, where the rainbow, known as Bifröst, serves as a link between Asgard (the realm of gods) and Midgard (the realm of humans).

Religious narratives across different faiths have also attributed significant meaning to the rainbow.

What does the rainbow represent in some other cultures:

Culturally, the rainbow has acquired various interpretations and symbolic associations. In many societies, it is seen as a sign of good fortune and blessings. For example, in Chinese culture, the rainbow is considered a bridge to connect mortal realms with the heavens, signifying auspicious events and harmonious unions. Indigenous cultures around the world often view the rainbow as a connection to their ancestral heritage, representing spiritual guidance, protection, and a harmonious relationship with nature.

The rainbow holds symbolic significance in various cultures around the world, often representing diverse meanings related to nature, spirituality, and folklore. Here are a few examples:

Norse Mythology, In Norse mythology, the rainbow bridge Bifröst connects the realm of the gods, Asgard, with Midgard, the realm of humans. The rainbow is seen as a pathway between these realms, symbolizing a connection between the mortal and divine worlds.

Native American Cultures, Several Native American tribes view the rainbow as a celestial bridge connecting different realms or dimensions. It is often associated with spiritual journeys, communication with ancestors, and blessings from the divine.

Chinese Culture, In Chinese folk lore, the rainbow is considered a bridge that links the human world with the heavens.

It is believed that spirits and immortals traverse this bridge, and the appearance of a rainbow is seen as an auspicious sign associated with good fortune and harmony.

In Yoruba culture and tradition, the rainbow, known as "Omi-Obi" or "Oju-Orun," holds symbolic significance and is associated with various meanings. In Yoruba cosmology, the rainbow is seen as a bridge between the earthly realm (Aye) and the spiritual realm (Orun), connecting the physical and metaphysical worlds.

Hawaiian Culture, In Hawaiian mythology, the rainbow is associated with the goddess of rain, Anuenue. The rainbow is considered a manifestation of her presence, and it is believed to bring blessings, healing, and protection.

Aboriginal Cultures, Indigenous Australian cultures have diverse interpretations of the rainbow. In some Aboriginal traditions, the rainbow serpent is a significant creation being associated with fertility, water, and life. The rainbow represents the serpent's pathway and is linked to the cycle of regeneration and the connection between land, water, and people.

These examples illustrate the rich and varied symbolism attributed to the rainbow across different cultures. The interpretations and meanings assigned to the rainbow in these cultures reflect their unique beliefs, mythologies, and spiritual frameworks. It highlights the universal fascination with this natural phenomenon and its ability to inspire wonder, spiritual connections, and cultural expressions across diverse communities.

Tracing the historical roots of rainbow symbolism reveals its significance in different time periods. Throughout history, the rainbow has been depicted in ancient art, such as frescoes and murals, showcasing its enduring impact on human creativity. It has also been referenced in ancient texts and literature, where its colors and beauty are described in poetic terms, symbolizing joy, beauty, and divine favor.

Today, the rainbow's historical and cultural significance continues to resonate. It has become a globally recognized symbol of unity, diversity, and hope. The rainbow flag, specifically, has emerged as an iconic symbol of the LGBTQ+ community, representing inclusivity, acceptance, and the fight for equal rights.

Understanding the historical and cultural significance of the rainbow allows us to appreciate its profound symbolism and universal appeal.

It invites us to embrace the beauty of the natural world and the connections between the divine, humans, and different cultures. The rainbow's timeless allure serves as a reminder of the enduring messages of hope, renewal, and harmony that it carries throughout history.

What does the rainbow represent in Islamic religion:

In Islamic religion, the rainbow holds a special significance and is seen as a symbol of hope, mercy, and divine beauty. The Quran, the holy book of Islam, mentions the rainbow as a sign of Allah's (God's) grace and a reminder of His covenant with humanity.

According to Islamic tradition, Prophet Noah (Nuh in Arabic) witnessed a great flood that covered the Earth as a divine punishment.

After the flood receded, Prophet Noah and his followers disembarked from the ark and saw a rainbow in the sky. The Quran describes this event in Surah Hud (Chapter 11), verse 41:

"And [Noah] said, 'Embark therein; in the name of Allah is its course and its anchorage. Indeed, my Lord is Forgiving and Merciful.' And it sailed with them through waves like mountains, and Noah called to his son who was apart [from them], 'O my son, come aboard with us and be not with the disbelievers.' [But] he said, 'I will take refuge on a mountain to protect me from the water.' [Noah] said, 'There is no protector today from the decree of Allah, except for whom He gives mercy.' And the waves came between them, and he was among the drowned. And it was said, 'O earth, swallow your water, and O sky, withhold [your rain].'

And the water subsided, and the matter was accomplished, and the ship came to rest on the [mountain of] Judiyy. And it was said, 'Away with the wrongdoing people.' And Noah called to his Lord and said, 'My Lord, indeed my son is of my family; and indeed, Your promise is true; and You are the most just of judges.'
He said, 'O Noah, indeed he is not of your family; indeed, he is [one whose] work was other than righteous, so ask Me not for that about which you have no knowledge. Indeed, I advise you, lest you be among the ignorant.' [Noah] said, 'My Lord, I seek refuge in You from asking that of which I have no knowledge. And unless You forgive me and have mercy upon me, I will be among the losers.'"

In this account, the rainbow serves as a sign of Allah's mercy and forgiveness, as well as a reminder of the consequences of wrongdoing.

It represents hope and the renewal of life after a calamity. It is a symbol of Allah's benevolence, providing reassurance to Prophet Noah and his followers after the devastating flood.

In Islamic culture, the rainbow is also regarded as a reflection of Allah's beautiful creation and a reminder of His power and majesty. It is often appreciated as a natural wonder and an expression of divine artistry.

It is important to note that Islamic interpretations of the rainbow may vary among different scholars and cultural contexts. However, the general understanding of the rainbow in Islam emphasizes its connection to Allah's mercy, hope, and beauty, as exemplified in the story of Prophet Noah.

What does the rainbow represents in Christian religion:

In Christian religion, the rainbow is associated with several significant themes and symbolisms found in the Bible, primarily related to God's promises, covenant, and divine presence.

The rainbow holds its most prominent symbolism in the Book of Genesis, where it is described as a sign of God's covenant with humanity following the great flood. According to the biblical account in Genesis 9:12-17, after the floodwaters receded, God established a covenant with Noah and all living creatures, promising never to destroy the Earth with a flood again. The rainbow is mentioned as a visible sign of this covenant:

"And God said, 'This is the sign of the covenant I am making between me and you and every living creature with you, a covenant for all generations to come:

I have set my rainbow in the clouds, and it will be the sign of the covenant between me and the earth. Whenever I bring clouds over the earth and the rainbow appears in the clouds, I will remember my covenant between me and you and all living creatures of every kind. Never again will the waters become a flood to destroy all life. Whenever the rainbow appears in the clouds, I will see it and remember the everlasting covenant between God and all living creatures of every kind on the earth.'" (Genesis 9:12-16, NIV)

The rainbow, in this context, represents God's faithfulness, mercy, and promise to preserve and protect His creation. It serves as a reminder of His enduring love and commitment to humanity and all living beings.

Additionally, the rainbow is associated with God's divine presence and glory. In the book of Ezekiel, the prophet describes a vision of God's appearance that includes a rainbow:

"Like the appearance of a rainbow in the clouds on a rainy day, so was the radiance around him. This was the appearance of the likeness of the glory of the Lord." (Ezekiel 1:28, NIV)

Here, the rainbow symbolizes the divine radiance and splendor surrounding God's presence. It signifies His majesty, holiness, and the awe-inspiring nature of His glory.

In Christian symbolism, the rainbow is often interpreted as a visual reminder of God's love, mercy, and faithfulness.

It serves as a testament to His unchanging nature and His desire for reconciliation with humanity. It also represents hope, redemption, and the promise of eternal life through Jesus Christ.

While the primary biblical references to the rainbow are related to God's covenant with humanity and His presence, it is important to note that interpretations and emphasis on the rainbow's symbolism may vary among different Christian denominations and theological perspectives.

Chapter 2:

Rainbow Symbolism in Religions and Spiritual Traditions

- Examining the rainbow's role in different religious traditions and its symbolism as a bridge between heaven and earth.
- Discussing the rainbow's representation of renewal, transformation, and the divine presence in various spiritual beliefs.
- Emphasizing the need to acknowledge and respect these spiritual interpretations alongside its association with the LGBT community.

Rainbow symbolism holds a significant place in religions and spiritual traditions worldwide, spanning across different cultures, beliefs, and time periods.

The rainbow's symbolic significance in these contexts reflects themes of divinity, harmony, and profound connections between the earthly and spiritual realms.

In numerous religious traditions, the rainbow is viewed as a bridge or conduit between heaven and earth, serving as a symbol of communication and interaction between the divine and humanity.

This symbolism is rooted in ancient myths, sacred texts, and spiritual teachings that highlight the rainbow's transcendent qualities.

In the Judeo-Christian tradition, for instance, the rainbow appears in the biblical narrative of Noah's Ark. Following the great flood, God places a rainbow in the sky as a sign of the covenant made with Noah, symbolizing divine protection and a promise to never again destroy the world by water.

The rainbow's presence represents divine grace, mercy, and a harmonious relationship between God and humanity.

Similarly, in Hinduism, the rainbow is associated with deities and cosmic harmony. In Hindu mythology, Indra, the king of gods, uses the rainbow as his celestial bow, connecting heaven and earth. The seven colors of the rainbow, known as VIBGYOR, are also linked to the seven chakras, or energy centers, within the human body, representing balance, spiritual growth, and alignment.

In Native American and indigenous cultures, the rainbow often symbolizes spiritual guidance, protection, and the connection between humans and the natural world. Native American tribes view the rainbow as a sign of unity and blessings, representing the divine's presence and favor. It is also seen as a pathway for spirits to travel between realms.

Beyond specific religious traditions, the rainbow holds broader spiritual symbolism as well. Its vibrant colors are often associated with divine attributes and qualities.

Red represents strength, vitality, and passion, while orange symbolizes creativity and transformation. Yellow embodies wisdom, joy, and enlightenment, while green represents growth, balance, and healing. Blue signifies truth, clarity, and spiritual insight, while indigo represents intuition and spiritual awareness. Violet or purple embodies spirituality, connection to higher realms, and divine consciousness.

The full spectrum of colors within the rainbow reflects the multifaceted nature of the divine and the infinite possibilities of spiritual growth and understanding.

The rainbow's symbolism in religions and spiritual traditions invites believers to contemplate the interconnectedness of all existence, to seek harmony and balance, and to acknowledge the divine presence in the world. It serves as a powerful reminder of the spiritual dimensions beyond the material realm and encourages individuals to cultivate a deeper connection with the divine, whether through prayer, meditation, or contemplation.

Exploring the rainbow's symbolism in religions and spiritual traditions reveals its profound significance as a sacred bridge, a divine covenant, and a representation of spiritual growth and enlightenment. Embracing this symbolism can inspire individuals to deepen their spiritual practices, cultivate a sense of unity and harmony, and embark on a journey of self-discovery and connection with the divine.

The rainbow holds deep spiritual interpretations that encompass themes of renewal, transformation, and divine connection. These interpretations are significant and should be acknowledged and respected alongside its association with the LGBT community.

Renewal is a fundamental aspect of the rainbow's symbolism. In various spiritual traditions, the rainbow represents a fresh start, a cleansing of the past, and the potential for new beginnings. It serves as a reminder that after periods of turmoil or darkness, there is always the opportunity for growth and positive change.

Just as the colors of the rainbow emerge after a storm, so too can individuals experience renewal and transformation in their lives.

Transformation is another core aspect of the rainbow's symbolism. The rainbow represents the transformative power of spiritual growth and inner evolution. Its vibrant colors signify the stages of personal development, from the foundational energies of red to the enlightened states of violet or purple. The rainbow encourages individuals to embark on a journey of self-discovery and spiritual advancement, embracing personal transformation and expanding their consciousness.

The rainbow's connection to the divine is a significant element in its symbolism. It represents a bridge between the earthly realm and the divine or spiritual realms. It serves as a reminder of our connection to something greater than ourselves, inviting individuals to acknowledge and nurture their relationship with the divine or the higher power of their understanding.

The rainbow's ethereal beauty embodies the presence of the divine in the world and encourages individuals to seek spiritual connection and guidance.

It is crucial to recognize and respect these spiritual interpretations of the rainbow alongside its association with the LGBT community. The rainbow flag, adopted by the LGBT community as a symbol of pride, diversity, and inclusivity, represents the struggles, resilience, and progress of the LGBTQ+ movement. The rainbow's association with the LGBT community does not diminish its spiritual symbolism but adds another layer of significance and meaning.

Acknowledging and respecting both the spiritual interpretations and the LGBT community's association with the rainbow allows for a broader understanding and appreciation of its symbolism.

It emphasizes the importance of inclusivity, diversity, and the recognition of different perspectives and experiences. By embracing these multiple interpretations, we foster an environment of respect, understanding, and unity, honoring both the spiritual and social dimensions of the rainbow's symbolism.

In conclusion, the rainbow holds profound spiritual interpretations, representing renewal, transformation, and divine connection. These spiritual meanings should be acknowledged and respected alongside its association with the LGBT community. Embracing both aspects of the rainbow's symbolism fosters inclusivity and understanding, reminding us of the importance of recognizing diverse interpretations and experiences.

Chapter 3:

The Rainbow as a Universal Symbol of Beauty and Diversity

- Exploring the rainbow as a celebration of the natural world's vibrant diversity.
- Examining the rainbow's aesthetic appeal and its influence on art, literature, and human creativity.
- Highlighting the importance of appreciating the rainbow's beauty beyond its symbolic association with the LGBT community.

The rainbow stands as a universal symbol of beauty and diversity, transcending cultural and geographical boundaries. It is a celebration of the natural world's vibrant spectrum and serves as a powerful reminder of the inherent diversity present in our environment.

The aesthetic appeal of the rainbow is undeniable. Its brilliant colors, gracefully arcing across the sky, evoke a sense of wonder and joy. Artists, poets, and writers have been inspired by the rainbow's visual splendor throughout history. Painters have sought to capture its radiant hues on canvas, while poets and writers have used it as a metaphor to convey emotions, experiences, and the richness of life. The rainbow's beauty has thus permeated various artistic expressions and served as a muse for human creativity.

Beyond its artistic influence, the rainbow holds profound significance in emphasizing the importance of diversity. Each color within the spectrum is distinct, yet together they create a harmonious whole. The rainbow reminds us that diversity is not only visually appealing but also essential for the overall balance and richness of our world.

It encourages us to appreciate and celebrate the unique qualities, perspectives, and experiences that each individual brings.

It is crucial to recognize and appreciate the beauty of the rainbow beyond its symbolic association with the LGBT community. While the rainbow flag has become an iconic symbol of pride, diversity, and inclusivity for the LGBTQ+ movement, the rainbow's beauty and symbolism extend far beyond this context. The rainbow is a testament to the diverse tapestry of life itself, encompassing a multitude of cultures, ethnicities, beliefs, and experiences.

By embracing the rainbow's universal symbolism of beauty and diversity, we foster a greater appreciation for the richness of our human family. It encourages us to celebrate and respect differences, fostering a more inclusive and harmonious society.

Recognizing the beauty of the rainbow beyond its association with any specific group allows us to connect on a deeper level, transcending boundaries and promoting understanding and acceptance.

In conclusion, the rainbow serves as a universal symbol of beauty and diversity. Its vibrant colors and graceful arcs remind us of the stunning variety found in the natural world. By appreciating the rainbow's aesthetic appeal and embracing its significance beyond its symbolic association with the LGBT community, we honor and celebrate the diversity that exists within our world. It is through this appreciation that we can foster an inclusive and harmonious society that values and respects the unique qualities and experiences of all individuals.

Chapter 4:

The LGBT Movement and the Rainbow's Adoption

- Tracing the origins of the rainbow flag as a symbol of the LGBT movement.
- Acknowledging the significance of the rainbow in promoting diversity, inclusivity, and equal rights.
- Raising awareness about the potential dangers of oversimplifying the rainbow's symbolism solely to the LGBT context.

The LGBT movement has adopted the rainbow as a powerful symbol of pride, diversity, and equal rights. The origins of the rainbow flag as an emblem for the LGBTQ+ community can be traced back to the late 1970s in San Francisco. Designed by artist Gilbert Baker, the flag was created to represent the diversity and unity within the LGBTQ+ community.

The rainbow flag quickly gained recognition and became an iconic symbol of the LGBT movement. Each color of the flag holds its own significance: red for life, orange for healing, yellow for sunlight, green for nature, blue for harmony, and violet for spirit. It represents the broad spectrum of identities and experiences within the community and serves as a visible symbol of pride, visibility, and inclusivity.

The adoption of the rainbow flag by the LGBT movement holds deep significance. It has played a pivotal role in promoting awareness, acceptance, and equal rights for the LGBTQ+ community. The flag serves as a rallying point, unifying diverse individuals under a shared symbol of pride and belonging. It has become a source of empowerment for LGBTQ+ individuals, encouraging self-acceptance and fostering a sense of community and support.

Moreover, the rainbow flag's association with the LGBT movement has helped raise global awareness of the struggles faced by the community and the importance of equality and inclusivity. It has been instrumental in advocating for LGBTQ+ rights, challenging discriminatory practices, and fostering social change. The rainbow flag has become a symbol of hope, resilience, and the ongoing fight for equal rights and acceptance.

However, it is essential to recognize the potential dangers of oversimplifying the rainbow's symbolism solely to the LGBT context.
The rainbow has a rich historical and cultural significance that extends beyond its association with any specific group. Oversimplification can lead to misunderstandings and dilute the broader symbolism of the rainbow.

The rainbow represents beauty, diversity, and interconnectedness in various religious, spiritual, and cultural contexts. It holds significance in mythology, folklore, and ancient traditions as a bridge between the earthly and divine realms, symbolizing hope, harmony, and renewal. By reducing the rainbow solely to its association with the LGBT movement, we risk overlooking the deeper layers of its symbolism and its universal appeal.

Raising awareness about the broader significance of the rainbow's symbolism encourages a more inclusive understanding of its meaning. Emphasizing that the rainbow represents not only the struggle for LGBTQ+ rights but also the celebration of diversity, equality, and the shared humanity of all individuals is crucial. This helps promote a greater appreciation for the rainbow's multifaceted symbolism and encourages respect for its historical, cultural, and spiritual interpretations.

In conclusion, the adoption of the rainbow flag by the LGBT movement has played a pivotal role in promoting diversity, inclusivity, and equal rights. It has become an iconic symbol of pride, visibility, and unity for the LGBTQ+ community. However, it is important to raise awareness about the dangers of oversimplifying the rainbow's symbolism solely to the LGBT context. Acknowledging the broader significance of the rainbow and its universal appeal fosters a more inclusive understanding and appreciation for its historical, cultural, and spiritual representations.

Chapter 5:

The Danger of Oversimplification and Exclusivity

- Examining the potential consequences of reducing the rainbow's symbolism exclusively to the LGBT movement.
- Discussing the unintentional erasure of other interpretations and cultural significance surrounding the rainbow.
- Addressing the potential impact on marginalized communities whose identities and struggles may be overshadowed.

The danger of oversimplification and exclusivity arises when the symbolism of the rainbow is reduced exclusively to the LGBT movement. While the rainbow flag has become an iconic representation of LGBTQ+ pride, it is crucial to recognize that the rainbow holds broader historical, cultural, and spiritual significance beyond this context.

By narrowly associating the rainbow solely with the LGBT movement, there is a risk of unintentionally erasing or overshadowing other interpretations and cultural significances surrounding the rainbow. The rainbow has been revered in various cultures, religions, and spiritual traditions throughout history, symbolizing diverse concepts such as divinity, renewal, and harmony.

 Failing to acknowledge these interpretations and cultural associations can lead to the marginalization of other communities and their respective struggles.

Oversimplification can perpetuate a limited understanding of the rainbow's symbolism, leading to the erasure of marginalized communities whose identities and struggles may be overshadowed.

It is important to recognize that the rainbow flag, while a powerful symbol for the LGBTQ+ community, should not overshadow or diminish the experiences and challenges faced by other marginalized groups, such as racial and ethnic minorities, individuals with disabilities, or those facing socio-economic inequality.

Inclusive dialogue and understanding are crucial to address this danger. It is essential to engage in conversations that recognize and respect the rainbow's broader symbolism and cultural significance.

 This includes acknowledging the historical roots of the rainbow in diverse cultures, appreciating its spiritual interpretations, and recognizing its connection to themes of diversity, equality, and inclusivity that extend beyond any specific community.

By promoting a more inclusive understanding of the rainbow's symbolism, we can celebrate and honor the struggles, identities, and experiences of all marginalized communities. This requires actively listening to and elevating the voices of those whose narratives may be overshadowed, ensuring that their stories and perspectives are given the attention they deserve.

Ultimately, it is crucial to recognize that the rainbow's symbolism is multifaceted and transcends any single association. By avoiding oversimplification and exclusivity, we can foster a more inclusive and compassionate society that appreciates the rich diversity of human experiences and honors the struggles faced by all marginalized communities.

Chapter 6:

Nuanced Conversations and Inclusivity

- Emphasizing the importance of nuanced conversations that honor the diverse interpretations of the rainbow.
- Encouraging understanding, respect, and inclusivity when discussing the rainbow's symbolism.
- Highlighting the need to embrace a broader perspective that recognizes and celebrates the richness and complexity of diverse symbolisms.

Engaging in nuanced conversations and fostering inclusivity when discussing the symbolism of the rainbow is of utmost importance. Such conversations recognize and honor the diverse interpretations of the rainbow, fostering understanding, respect, and a broader perspective.

It is crucial to understand that the rainbow carries a multitude of meanings across different cultures, religions, and spiritual traditions. By embracing nuanced conversations, we can appreciate the richness and complexity of these interpretations, recognizing that there is no singular or definitive understanding of the rainbow's symbolism.

Nuanced conversations invite us to listen actively and attentively to different perspectives, experiences, and cultural contexts associated with the rainbow.

This allows for a more comprehensive understanding of its symbolism and prevents the oversimplification or exclusion of certain interpretations.

Inclusive discussions surrounding the rainbow's symbolism require openness, empathy, and respect.

This entails creating a safe and welcoming space where individuals from diverse backgrounds can share their insights and contribute to the conversation. Active listening, without judgment or preconceived notions, is crucial to fostering inclusivity and understanding.

Moreover, embracing a broader perspective is essential. Recognizing and celebrating the richness and complexity of diverse symbolisms associated with the rainbow allows us to appreciate the multiplicity of meanings it holds. This means acknowledging the significance of the rainbow in religious and spiritual narratives, cultural traditions, folklore, and historical contexts.By expanding our understanding and embracing diverse interpretations, we create room for dialogue that celebrates the rainbow's symbolism in all its facets.
In doing so, we acknowledge the importance of inclusivity, diversity, and respect for different perspectives and experiences.

Nuanced conversations and inclusivity also help us avoid inadvertently overshadowing or erasing the experiences and struggles of marginalized communities.

By actively engaging with diverse voices, we ensure that all narratives are given space and consideration. This helps prevent the perpetuation of harmful stereotypes or the marginalization of any group.

In conclusion, fostering nuanced conversations and promoting inclusivity when discussing the symbolism of the rainbow is crucial. This requires embracing a broader perspective that recognizes and celebrates the richness and complexity of diverse interpretations. By engaging in these conversations with openness, empathy, and respect, we create a platform for understanding, appreciation, and dialogue that honors the multifaceted nature of the rainbow's symbolism.

Chapter 7:

Moving Forward: Appreciating the Multifaceted Rainbow

- Summarizing the key points of the book and the importance of embracing the rainbow's diverse meanings.
- Encouraging readers to engage in thoughtful dialogue and to consider the potential risks of oversimplification.
- Promoting inclusivity, understanding, and respect for the rainbow's universal symbolism.

"Moving Forward: Appreciating the Multifaceted Rainbow" encapsulates the key points of our exploration into the diverse meanings of the rainbow. Throughout this book, we have delved into its historical, cultural, and spiritual significance, discussed its representation in various contexts, and examined its association with the LGBT movement. Now, as we conclude, it is important to emphasize the importance of embracing the rainbow's multifaceted nature.

The rainbow is a symbol that transcends boundaries and connects us to the beauty and diversity of the natural world. Its vibrant colors and graceful arc inspire awe and wonder. We have explored its representation as a symbol of renewal, transformation, and divinity, reminding us of the constant cycles of life and the harmony that exists within the universe.

However, it is crucial to acknowledge that the rainbow's symbolism extends beyond any single interpretation or association. We have discussed the potential risks of oversimplification, particularly when reducing its significance solely to the LGBT context. Oversimplification can unintentionally erase other cultural interpretations and overshadow the struggles of marginalized communities. By recognizing the rainbow's broader meanings, we can foster inclusivity and ensure that all narratives are respected and honored.

To appreciate the multifaceted rainbow, it is essential to engage in thoughtful dialogue. By actively listening to diverse perspectives, we expand our understanding and deepen our appreciation for the richness of its symbolism. Thoughtful dialogue encourages us to consider the potential impact of our words and actions, promoting empathy, understanding, and respect.

In our pursuit of inclusivity, it is vital to celebrate the rainbow's universal symbolism. Beyond any single association, the rainbow represents the beauty of diversity and the interconnectedness of all individuals. By embracing this universal aspect, we foster a society that values and respects the unique qualities, perspectives, and experiences of all people.

As we move forward, let us remember the importance of appreciating the multifaceted rainbow. By engaging in nuanced conversations, considering the potential risks of oversimplification, and promoting inclusivity, understanding, and respect, we can truly honor the rainbow's universal symbolism. It is through this appreciation that we foster a world where diversity is celebrated, understanding is cultivated, and all individuals are treated with dignity and equality.

Conclusion:

- Providing a final reflection on the exploration of rainbow symbolism and the potential dangers of using it exclusively for the LGBT movement.
- Encouraging readers to continue exploring and appreciating the rich tapestry of meanings associated with the rainbow while fostering inclusivity and understanding.

Throughout our exploration of rainbow symbolism, we have delved into its historical, cultural, and spiritual significance, acknowledging its association with the LGBT movement while also recognizing the dangers of exclusively limiting its meaning to this context. As we conclude our journey, it is important to provide a final reflection on these aspects.

The rainbow holds a diverse range of meanings that span across cultures and time. It represents the beauty of diversity, the interconnectedness of life, and the renewal and transformation inherent in the natural world. While the rainbow has become a powerful symbol of pride, visibility, and inclusivity for the LGBT movement, it is crucial to be aware of the potential dangers of using it exclusively in this context.

Using the rainbow exclusively for the LGBT movement may inadvertently overshadow or diminish the broader historical and cultural interpretations associated with it. By narrowing its symbolism, we risk erasing the rich tapestry of meanings that exist across different religious, spiritual, and mythological traditions. This erasure can marginalize other communities and overlook the struggles they face, inadvertently perpetuating inequality and exclusion.

It is essential to engage in nuanced conversations and embrace a broader perspective that honors and respects the multifaceted nature of the rainbow's symbolism. By recognizing its diverse interpretations, we create space for understanding and appreciation, promoting inclusivity and avoiding the risk of oversimplification.

Moreover, an exclusive focus on the rainbow's association with the LGBT movement can sometimes lead to a misperception that the struggles faced by other marginalized communities are overshadowed or disregarded. It is crucial to remember that there are multiple intersecting identities and experiences that must be acknowledged and supported. By recognizing and addressing the unique challenges faced by various marginalized groups, we can foster a more inclusive and equitable society.

In conclusion, as we reflect on our exploration of rainbow symbolism, we must recognize the potential dangers of exclusively using it for the LGBT movement. By appreciating the richness and complexity of its meanings across cultures, religions, and traditions, we ensure that the rainbow's symbolism is not diminished or confined to one interpretation. Through inclusive dialogue, understanding, and respect, we can navigate these complexities, promoting a more inclusive society that values the diverse experiences and struggles of all individuals.

As we conclude our exploration of the rich tapestry of meanings associated with the rainbow, I encourage you, the reader, to continue your own journey of discovery and appreciation. The rainbow's symbolism is vast and diverse, reaching across cultures, religions, and historical contexts.

By delving deeper into its multifaceted meanings, you can expand your understanding and embrace the beauty of its universal significance.

In your exploration, it is important to foster inclusivity and understanding. Engage in conversations that honor diverse perspectives and experiences. Listen attentively to the narratives of different cultures, religions, and marginalized communities.

By actively seeking out and learning from these diverse voices, you can broaden your understanding of the rainbow's symbolism and cultivate empathy and respect for others.

Recognize the potential dangers of exclusivity and oversimplification. Avoid reducing the rainbow's meaning solely to one association or context.

Embrace the complexity and richness of its interpretations, acknowledging the historical, cultural, and spiritual significances it holds. By doing so, you contribute to a more inclusive understanding and appreciation of the rainbow's symbolism.

Celebrate the diversity and interconnectedness that the rainbow represents. Appreciate the beauty and vibrancy it brings to our world.

Allow its symbolism to inspire you to foster unity, acceptance, and equality in your own life and in society. Embrace the rainbow as a reminder of the importance of valuing and respecting the uniqueness of each individual.

Continuing your exploration of the rainbow's meanings and fostering inclusivity and understanding will not only deepen your own knowledge but also contribute to a more compassionate and harmonious world. By embracing the rainbow's symbolism in all its richness, you can play a part in creating a society that appreciates diversity, celebrates unity, and treats all individuals with dignity and respect.

So, I invite you to embark on this ongoing journey of exploration, appreciating the vast array of meanings associated with the rainbow. Let us continue to learn, grow, and contribute to a world where the beauty and diversity of the rainbow are cherished and celebrated by all.